Dinosaur Herds

by Tim Glazer
illustrated by Burgandy Beam

Editorial Offices: Glenview, Illinois • Parsippany, New Jersey • New York, New York
Sales Offices: Needham, Massachusetts • Duluth, Georgia • Glenview, Illinois
Coppell, Texas • Sacramento, California • Mesa, Arizona

Dinosaurs don't live now.
They did live in the past.
These dinosaurs did live alone.

Many dinosaurs did live in herds.
In herds, many animals live together.

Dinosaur herds could work together.
This herd made a circle.
The baby dinosaurs went inside.
There they could be safe.

Dinosaur herds could hunt together.
This herd will push the big dinosaur down.
It will be their dinner.

Dinosaur herds could make nests together.
This herd made a nest for eggs.
The big dinosaur kept the nest safe.

Dinosaurs don't live now.
They did live in the past.
These dinosaurs did live in herds.